D1117215

MEGASTARS™

RIHANNA

BRIDGET HEOS

rosen publishing's
rosen
central®

New York

For Hannah

Published in 2011 by The Rosen Publishing Group, Inc.
29 East 21st Street, New York, NY 10010

First Edition

Library of Congress Cataloging-in-Publication Data

Heos, Bridget.
Rihanna / Bridget Heos. — 1st ed.
    p. cm. — (Megastars)
Includes bibliographical references and index.
ISBN 978-1-4358-3576-4 (library binding)
ISBN 978-1-4488-2262-1 (pbk.)
ISBN 978-1-4488-2268-3 (6-pack)
1. Rihanna, 1988–Juvenile literature. 2. Singers–Biography–Juvenile literature. I. Title.
ML3930.R44H46 2011
782.42164092–dc22

                                              2010021321

Manufactured in the United States of America

CPSIA Compliance Information: Batch #W11YA: For further information, contact Rosen Publishing, New York, New York, at 1-800-237-9932.

On the cover: Rihanna's personal style, from her hairstyles to her flamboyant outfits, generates a lot of buzz.

CONTENTS

Few artists are recognizable by their first name only. Rihanna is one of them. As a young girl growing up in Barbados, an island in the West Indies, she dreamed of becoming a star in America. Her dream came true when a producer discovered her while vacationing on the island. Rihanna signed her first record deal at age sixteen and has put out a chart-topping new album every year since.

After charming listeners with her catchy dance beats and soaring vocals, Rihanna transformed into an edgier artist— both in look and style. Although her third album was

Rihanna signed her first record deal, for Music of the Sun, at age six-teen. She returned home to Barbados on April 22, 2006, for a party to celebrate the release of her next album, A Girl Like Me.

titled *Good Girl Gone Bad*, Rihanna was, in truth, still a nice girl from Barbados. Her best friends were childhood buddies. And she continued to work hard and avoid the Hollywood party scene.

Her beauty, poise, and success seemed to indicate a perfect life. So fans were shocked when, in February of 2009, Rihanna was the victim of physical abuse at the hands of her then boyfriend, Chris Brown. Instead of talking to the press right away, the singer turned to the studio. Depicting the anger, sadness, and strength of somebody hurt by a loved one, *Rated R* was released to critical acclaim. Today, Rihanna is a singer, style icon, and role model for young girls. Although she's already put out four albums, she is still a young woman with a long career ahead of her.

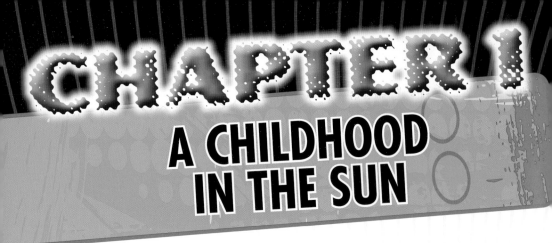

CHAPTER 1

A CHILDHOOD IN THE SUN

Robyn Rihanna Fenty was born on February 20, 1988, in Barbados, an island in the Caribbean Sea. Her father, Ronald, was a warehouse supervisor of African and Irish heritage. Her mother, Monica, was an accountant of Guyanese descent.

Rihanna, her parents, and her two younger brothers, Rajad and Rorrey, lived in a lower-middle-class neighborhood, but Rihanna never felt poor. In a November 3, 2009, *Glamour* interview, she said, "My mother never made us feel that way. She loved me unconditionally. She made us feel anything was possible and instilled in me such confidence."

Still, Rihanna's home life was difficult. Her father was addicted to drugs. Rihanna told Diane Sawyer in a *20/20* interview on November 7, 2009, that he physically abused her mother. Her mother hid it, but Rihanna knew. At night she lay awake, afraid that they would fight. When they did, she would try to stand in the middle. She told Sawyer that she remembers thinking, "I'm never going to date someone like my dad, never."

The stressful home life affected Rihanna physically. At age eight, she began having headaches. They were so bad that doctors ordered a CAT scan to check for a brain tumor. Nothing turned up. When Rihanna was fourteen, her parents divorced. At that point, the headaches went away.

Rihanna remains close to her two brothers, including Rajad, pictured here with his older sister at the People Music Lounge on August 14, 2007.

For a time, Rihanna and her father became friends. She told *Elle* on May 4, 2008, "Now my dad is like the coolest person on the planet. He doesn't smother me. He lets me live my life. And he's been like that a lot, even when I was younger. He would watch me making a mistake and he wouldn't stop me. My dad, he lets me make it and then I learn." Later, the father-daughter relationship fell apart, and they were no longer on speaking terms. However, Rihanna remained close to her mother and brothers.

During her childhood, Rihanna kept her worries to herself. Singing provided an outlet. She sang all the time: to her cousins, her stuffed animals, and even her pillows. She dreamed of being a star.

As a teenager, she attended Combermere Secondary School, a high school that dates back to the 1600s. While there, she made her mark. She performed Mariah Carey's "Hero" at a school talent contest. She won a school beauty pageant. She formed a band with two schoolmates. She wanted to leave Barbados to become a star in America. But her mother said she had to stay in school until she got a record contract.

At fifteen, her dream was about to come true. Music producer Evan Rogers and his wife, Jackie, were vacationing in Barbados, where Jackie was from. Rogers had produced songs for NSYNC, Christina Aguilera, and Jessica Simpson. As a favor to a friend, he agreed to watch Rihanna and her band perform.

When he first saw Rihanna, he thought that if she had a good voice, she could become a star. She sang "Dangerously in Love" by Beyoncé and "Emotion" by Destiny's Child. Rogers thought that, like many young singers, she copied other artists (in her case, Beyoncé and Mariah Carey) too much. But he could also tell she had talent of her own.

Rogers asked Rihanna to come to Connecticut with him and his wife. Rihanna begged her mother to let her go, but her mother was nervous. She didn't know Evan Rogers and his wife very well. However,

Jay-Z, pictured here with Rihanna (left) and musical artist Teairra Mari
(right), had recently become president of Def Jam Records when he
heard Rihanna's demo tape. He set up a meeting with her right away.

it eased her mind to learn that Jackie was from Barbados. She let Rihanna go with them.

At the time, Rihanna was very shy. Evan and Jackie were like second parents to her. With Evan and his business partner Carl Sturken, she recorded a demo. Demos are samples of musical artists' work—a few songs to illustrate their style and talent. After recording the demo, she returned home to Barbados.

Rogers sent the demo to record labels, including Def Jam Records. There, it reached the hands of Jay-Z. As a talented young rapper, Jay-Z had founded Roc-A-Fella Records to produce his own music. In 2004, he temporarily retired from recording to become president of Def Jam Records. Soon after taking the helm, he became known for discovering young talent. He fostered the careers of Young Jeezy and Teairra Mari, among others. With Rihanna, he liked what he heard. He set up a meeting with her and her representatives right away.

TURN THE MUSIC UP

Rihanna flew to New York to try out for Jay-Z at Def Jam Records. The night before the audition, she couldn't sleep. She tried on several outfits and styles of makeup. She pictured what a top music mogul like Jay-Z must look like while auditioning a new artist. She imagined he'd be wearing a fancy suit and smoking a cigar.

Upon reaching the offices of Jay-Z, she saw that he wasn't dressed in the intimidating manner she'd imagined. Instead, he wore a T-shirt and tennis shoes. But that did little to ease her mind. Her career was at stake. Before the audition, she was shaking. Then she started to sing "For the Love of You," by Whitney Houston. The nerves melted away. She gave it everything she had.

Afterward, she couldn't believe that she had just performed for Jay-Z. She was nervous once again. Luckily, Jay-Z had liked what he heard.

BARBADOS: ISLAND OF THE SUN

Barbados is the eastern-most Caribbean island. Just 166 square miles (431 square kilometers), if it were a perfect square, it would be only about 13 miles (21 km) long and 13 miles wide. The country is home to approximately 284,600 people. Barbados has a tropical climate, with a rainy season from June to October. Hurricanes rarely make landfall.

When the British landed on Barbados in 1627, it was uninhabited. They brought slaves—mainly from West Africa, but also from Ireland, Scotland, and England, to work the sugar plantations. Slavery was abolished in 1834, but Britain continued to rule. Independence was declared in 1966. English is the official language.

Today, most Barbadians are descendants of slaves brought to the island. Education is free in Barbados—not only for children but also for university students, which means Barbados has a well-educated population. According to The CIA World Factbook, 99.7 percent of the population age fifteen and up can read, giving the island a higher literacy rate than the United States.

Sugar continues to be a big business, but, today, tourism is the top industry. Along with offshore banking, it has fostered a strong economy. Though the country has its share of poverty, in general it has a relatively high standard of living.

So had everybody else. In fact, they were so taken with Rihanna that they practically put Def Jam on lockdown. Rihanna wasn't allowed to leave until everybody had signed a contract. Twelve hours later—in the wee hours of the morning—her lawyers finished working out a deal. Rihanna signed to Def Jam Records at age sixteen.

This was a coup. Many young and talented singers dream of getting a record deal (the lines at *American Idol* tryouts testify to that). Few actually get signed. Those who do often don't make it for long in the business. They don't sell enough records. Their singles don't get airtime.

Bob Marley, shown here performing in 1976, popularized reggae music—a mix of Jamaican and R&B sounds—in the United States. Critics called Rihanna's first album a mix of Caribbean and pop beats.

Rihanna was an exception to the rule. In 2005, just seven months after signing with Def Jam, her first album, *Music of the Sun*, was released. Critics called it a mix of pop, reggae, dancehall, and soca.

Pop, or popular, music draws from rock 'n' roll, soul, R&B, and rap, and it appeals to a large audience, particularly of young people. It is the music heard on the radio again and again.

Reggae is a mix of traditional Jamaican music and R&B. Jamaican artists like Bob Marley and Peter Tosh popularized the music in America in the 1960s. Dancehall (also known as ragga) is a faster, more contemporary form of reggae.

Soca stands for soul calypso. It originated in the 1970s as a rock 'n' roll version of calypso, a traditional musical style in the Caribbean. Very popular in the Caribbean, soca is best known in America for the songs "Hot Hot Hot," originally by Arrow but made famous by Buster Poindexter, and "Who Let the Dogs Out" originally by Anselm Douglas and popularized by the Baha Men.

Rihanna's "Pon de Replay," an upbeat dance song, was the first breakout single on *Music of the Sun*. It climbed the Billboard Hot 100 to number 2. The song "If It's Lovin' That You Want" also reached the Top 40. Rihanna didn't write these songs, but her unique voice and powerful persona brought them to life. *Music of the Sun* sold two million copies.

When "Pon de Replay" reached the top 10, Jay-Z told Rihanna not to get used to that kind of overnight success; it usually didn't happen. He also cautioned her to stay humble and to always be a good person. She listened to his advice even as her career soared to new heights.

CHAPTER 2

GOOD GIRL GONE BAD

Just eight months after *Music of the Sun* came out, Rihanna's second album, *A Girl Like Me*, was released. It produced even more hits. "SOS," which sampled "Tainted Love," was used in a Nike commercial. "Unfaithful," a twist on the typical infidelity song since it came from the point of view of the cheater, was a top single. Rihanna was named the 2006 Female Artist of the Year at the Billboard Music Awards. Capitalizing on her success, she started the Believe Foundation, which helps children around the world get the medical help they need.

While the public loved Rihanna, critics were skeptical. They knew she had the look and the voice. But did she have the depth to become a great star? For one thing, she didn't write her own music. For *A Girl Like Me*, Evan Rogers and producers and lyricists at Def Jam wrote the songs. Rihanna had some input, and Rogers believed she had writing talent, but Rihanna wasn't considered a singer-songwriter like Gwen Stefani, at the time, or Lady Gaga, today.

Other singers who didn't write their own songs, such as Celine Dion, managed to garner respect for their artistry. They put their heart and soul into their music and chose songs that spoke to who they were. Critics wondered whether Rihanna would become a songwriter, a singer known for her dramatic artistry, or neither.

Rihanna was also taking hits from the entertainment media in her personal life. There were rumors that she was dating Jay-Z, who at

Rihanna performed in New York on April 9, 2008, to benefit her charity for children in need, Believe. Afterward, she met young fan Daniel Fratto.

the time was dating Beyoncé. (The two are now married.) At first, Rihanna thought it was funny—like an outlandish high school rumor. But the rumor persisted. Rihanna and Jay-Z denied it, and being in the spotlight, Rihanna learned to ignore what people said.

Cosmopolitan asked Rihanna about her personal relationships in March 2008. She said that although she wasn't dating anyone at the time, she knew what kind of girlfriend she would want to be: one with high expectations.

"Here's the key," she told *Cosmopolitan*, "You can't lower your standards for a guy because he won't respect you and he'll tell his friends. You always have to stick up for yourself and speak your mind."

Not only did she set the record straight in her personal life, she was also silencing the doubts of music critics. In 2007, Rihanna released

Rihanna, sporting a new stylish haircut called the Chinese bob, signs copies of *Good Girl Gone Bad* on June 5, 2007, in Universal City, California.

Good Girl Gone Bad. Not yet twenty years old, Rihanna still didn't write the songs herself or delve too deeply emotionally. But with powerful beats and amazing vocals, it was considered her best album yet.

At this point, like many female singers who begin their careers as teens, she shed her good girl image for an edgier one. (Britney Spears and Christina Aguilera are other examples of stars who followed the "good girl gone bad" playbook.) Rihanna said that this new style spoke more to who she really was. Her label had pushed for the sweet style of her earlier two albums. (They even told her that her lipstick had to be natural—not bright pink or red!) She, on the other hand, had wanted to be on the cutting edge of fashion and music. Now, that's just what she did.

She changed her clothing style from a teenage, beachy look to a fashion forward, urban look. Designers like Zac Posen and Dan and Dean Caten wanted her to not only wear their clothing, but also to model it at fashion events. They considered her to be one of the only nonprofessional models who could show off a new look. The Catens wanted so badly for her to model their Dsquared2 clothing line in their Fall 2007 Milan show that they changed the date so that she could appear on the catwalk. She flew in for the show and immediately returned to Canada for a concert tour.

For *Good Girl Gone Bad*, she also did something that most girls consider a big risk: she cut her hair really short.

THE RIHANNA

Rihanna kept telling her managers she was going to chop off her locks. They didn't believe her. Still, they nervously asked, "How short?" Then, the night before the photo shoot for the *Good Girl Gone Bad* album cover, she had her hair bobbed and dyed black. The first time the people at Def Jam saw her new look was when they received the album cover. They loved it. So did lots of other people.

Showcasing a new hairstyle that is now known as "the Rihanna," Rihanna appears at the Palais des Festivals in Cannes, France, on January 26, 2008.

Before the 2008 NRJ Music Awards in Cannes, France, Rihanna had her hair cut even shorter. That look became known in hair salons as "the Rihanna." Having a hairstyle named for you is a rare tribute only a handful of stars have attained (as in Jennifer Aniston's "the Rachel" and Victoria Beckham's "Bob It Like Beckham," also known as "the Pob.")

Musicwise, Rihanna sought a grittier sound. To accomplish that, she turned to producers like Timbaland, who created "Lemme Get That," and Ne-Yo, who wrote, "Good Girl Gone Bad" and "Take a Bow." The most famous song on the album, "Umbrella," was written by Terius "The-Dream" Nash.

The new image and sound paid off. *Good Girl Gone Bad* sold 4 million copies, and 2.2 million people downloaded "Umbrella." "Don't Stop the Music" became the new party anthem. "Take a Bow" became the ultimate kiss-off song. And, of course, "Good Girl Gone Bad" was a breakout hit, too.

But what exactly did it mean for a good girl to go bad? For Rihanna, it didn't mean she went wild. She didn't like to hang out in the Hollywood club scene. She did travel with an entourage, but it was a group she trusted, and it included Melissa Forde, her best friend since they were kids in Barbados. Their idea of a good time was going to the drug store, buying a bunch of new makeup, and trying it out. Rihanna also liked pulling off innocent pranks—like putting a drop of lemon juice in a friend's mouth while she slept, so that she'd wake up tasting something sour. She stayed close to her family, too, with her brothers sometimes accompanying her to photo shoots.

Some might say Rihanna went "bad" as in the Michael Jackson song "Bad." She became the best at her craft, and in doing so, grew more confident in herself. She was no longer the shy girl. She was now involved in her career and business decisions. She was also becoming a household name.

In 2007, Rihanna became the face of Cover Girl Cosmetics. The next year, she appeared in *People*'s Most Beautiful issue

RIHANNA'S CHANGING HAIRSTYLES

Rihanna became a star at sixteen. With the release of Music of the Sun, she wore her hair long and wavy, a popular look among teens. It was brown with golden highlights. The next year, when A Girl Like Me came out, Rihanna kept her long tresses but began experimenting with length and color. At the 2006 Billboard Music Awards, for instance, she wore it below her waist and very dark brown.

Then, with the release of Good Girl Gone Bad in 2007, Rihanna shocked everyone by cutting her hair short. Her asymmetrical bob—short in the back and angled to be longer in the front—was an edgier look. Also, her hair color was now black. Soon after, she added bangs and went for a more even bob—a look called a Chinese bob.

The next year, she cut her hair even shorter for the 2008 NRJ Music Awards. Now it was short and layered in the back, and longer in the front (it came down over her eyes.) The new look was so popular that people began asking for "the Rihanna" at hair salons. She kept her hair short, but later dyed it honey blond for her Rated R tour.

(ironically, without makeup). She also graced the covers of Cosmopolitan and Elle.

Beyond the music and glamour, she began reading movie scripts and taking acting lessons. (She appeared on the soap opera All My Children and hoped to star in an action film.) She also continued her work with the Believe Foundation. In February 2008, Rihanna learned of a mother, Lisa Gershowitz Flynn, in New York who had leukemia. Without a bone marrow transplant, she would die. Through Believe, Rihanna began working with the charity DKMS, the largest bone marrow donor center in the world, to find donors for Flynn and others.

The same year, Rihanna won a Video Music Award and a Grammy (best rap/sung collaboration) for "Umbrella." Onstage, Jay-Z, who rapped in the song, humorously "translated" for her as she accepted the award. He was pretending people couldn't understand her through her Barbados accent.

Rihanna performs "Umbrella" from her Good Girl Gone Bad *album at the MTV Movie Awards on June 3, 2007. The song won a Grammy for best rap/sung collaboration.*

In spite of the awards, those in Rihanna's circle knew she would need to dig deeper emotionally to advance artistically. Jay-Z said that even though she was blowing people away with her talent, she needed to let people know her as a person, as artists like Mary J. Blige had done. He said she would need to decide what her story and her struggle were and tell that story. Rogers said that he hoped Rihanna would cowrite her next album. He said she was talented melodically, and he agreed that she needed to tell her own story.

CHAPTER 3

DON'T STOP THE MUSIC

Rihanna was on top of the world. Careerwise, the sky was the limit. In spite of her celebrity, she had remained a nice, down-to-earth person. Romantically, things seemed to be going well, too. She began dating eighteen-year-old Chris Brown, an R&B singer. He seemed like a catch. They had been good friends since he was fifteen and she was sixteen. He didn't drink or do drugs. He made her feel like a kid again. They also shared the experience of being stars at a young age. At one point, her song, "Don't Stop the Music," made it to number 3, right after Chris Brown's "With You."

But things weren't exactly as they seemed. Rihanna would later say that Brown had control issues. Police reports also indicate an incident where he broke her windshield, and another in which he shoved her into a wall. However, what happened on February 8, 2009, totally shocked her.

Later, Rihanna would describe that scary night to Diane Sawyer on 20/20: Brown and Rihanna had attended a Grammy Awards party the night before the awards show. Everything had gone well. But as Brown was driving them home, Rihanna saw a text message from his former girlfriend. She kept asking him about the message and didn't think he was being straight with her.

Soon, he snapped. He shoved her against the window. Her mouth filled with blood. He punched her. He said verbally abusive things to her.

Rihanna and Chris Brown, shown here at Z100's Jingle Ball in New York on December 16, 2005, had been good friends since she was sixteen and he was fifteen. They later began dating.

She recalled, "He had no soul in his eyes, just blank. So at that point, I just didn't know what could happen. He was clearly just blacked out. It was almost like he had nothing to lose. He has so much to lose."

He kept driving into a residential neighborhood. She tried to call her assistant but couldn't. He had her in a headlock—she struggled to breathe. He bit her ear and finger. She kept thinking, "When will it stop?"

She was screaming. She didn't realize it, but someone inside a house had heard her. They didn't come out, but they called the police. By the time they arrived, Brown had fled the scene.

When Rihanna went to the police station, her eyes were practically swollen shut. Her mouth was also swollen. Her forehead was badly bruised. Besides being physically wounded, she felt embarrassed.

Rihanna and Brown were both scheduled to perform at the Grammys. Instead, Brown turned himself into the police on charges of making criminal threats. The police were also considering domestic violence charges. Rihanna also declined to appear at the awards show but did not comment on Brown's arrest.

Soon, someone leaked the photo taken of Rihanna after the attack to the media, which later sparked an internal investigation by the Los Angeles Police Department. On February 19, TMZ published the photo on its Web site. Although Rihanna was almost unrecognizable because of her swollen eyes and battered face, a tattoo on her neck showed that it was likely her. Adding insult to injury, her personal tragedy was now entertainment news.

After the incident, helicopters swarmed her home and around a hundred people descended on her cul de sac. Rihanna would now be forced to respond to the attack in a very public way.

RUSSIAN ROULETTE

At first, Rihanna didn't talk to the media. She wasn't ready to talk about the attack. But others had plenty to say. For many, it was a

Rihanna, pictured with attorney Donald Etra, appeared in court on June 22, 2009, for Chris Brown's felony assault hearing. Brown pleaded guilty to the assault charge.

chance to shed light on something lurking under the radar: dating violence—especially among teens. On March 12, *The Oprah Show* discussed the problem, stating that an estimated one in three high school girls had been or would be involved in an abusive relationship. Winfrey encouraged parents and teens to talk about the issue. "Love doesn't hurt," she said. "And if a man hits you once, he will hit you again."

While voices of reason spoke out against abuse, a few people blamed Rihanna for what happened. Some teens featured on *Oprah* said that they thought she had hit him first and therefore deserved to be beaten. (Neither Rihanna nor Chris Brown have said that Rihanna struck Brown. Rihanna has said that even if she had, it wouldn't mean she should be brutally attacked.)

TEEN ABUSE

In America, 1.5 million women are raped or assaulted by their partners every year, according to The Oprah Show. *Teenagers are no exception. It's estimated that one in three teenage girls have or will experience dating abuse. While abuse seems like an obvious deal breaker, it doesn't always lead to a breakup. The young woman may feel too beaten down to make her move, she may be in denial about the danger of her situation, or she may love the abuser too much to leave. It may take a woman several instances of abuse before she'll leave. Here are some warning signs of an abusive relationship:*

- *He tells you who you can and can't talk to.*
- *He coerces or forces you to do things you don't want to do.*
- *He makes you feel guilty for small things like not responding immediately to a text or for spending time with someone other than him.*
- *You have a bad feeling in your gut about how things are going.*

Rihanna has said that she knows this wasn't her fault. Still, she felt bad for Chris Brown. He had issued an apology, but many of his fans now hated him. Many radio stations had stopped playing his songs. Rihanna knew how badly she felt as the victim of abuse. How badly must the abuser feel? She worried that he would hurt himself. So she went back to him. On February 27, *People* reported that Rihanna and Brown were spending time together in Miami Beach.

She later explained to Diane Sawyer that she had been in denial about what happened. "You want this thing to go away," she said. "This is a memory you don't ever want to happen again."

But Rihanna soon realized that it had happened, and nothing could undo it. She discovered that everything about Brown now annoyed her. She resented him for how he had hurt her—both physically and emotionally.

She also told Sawyer that she realized that because this story was playing out in the media, she had a responsibility to the girls who were watching. She knew that her decision—in the name of love and forgiveness—could result in a young girl getting killed.

Through tears, she said, "I couldn't be held responsible for telling them to go back. If Chris never hit me again, who's to say their boyfriend won't? Who's to say they won't kill these girls?" She left Brown and returned to Los Angeles.

On August 25, 2009, under a plea bargain, Brown received 5 years probation and 180 hours of community service for felony assault. He was also ordered to take a domestic violence class and to stay at least 100 yards (91.4 meters) away from Rihanna for five years except at music industry events. Some people sympathized with Brown, citing a cycle of abuse that stemmed from his mother being abused by his stepfather when Brown was a child. (The stepfather denies the claims.) Some fans accepted his apology. They believed he was trying to do better.

But Rihanna told Sawyer. "I just didn't know if he understood the extent of what he did. The face, the broken arm, the black eye, it's going to heal. That's not the problem. It's the scar inside . . . I don't think he understood that. They never do."

All of these feelings came out several months after the attack. At the time, Rihanna didn't even like to talk to friends about what happened. It made them feel too sad, and that made her feel sadder than she already was. But she did want to tell her story. So she wrote it in songs.

It wasn't the story Evan Rogers or Jay-Z had wanted her to have to tell. But it was the story she had to tell. About a month after the attack, she returned to the studio, this time, to write many of her own songs.

CHAPTER 4

COLD CASE LOVE

For Rihanna, working on a new album was therapy. The microphone didn't judge her or feel bad for her. She could say whatever she wanted. Rihanna collaborated with Ne-Yo, Justin Timberlake, and Jeezy to write songs that expressed what she was going through.

"Cold Case Love," which Rihanna cowrote with Justin Timberlake, talks about leaving an abusive relationship. She addresses the song to a guy, saying that he committed a crime against her. She sings that she went back to him one more time but won't make that mistake again. Rihanna has said that everything she didn't say after the Chris Brown attack is in this song.

In contrast, "Russian Roulette," which Ne-Yo wrote and produced, describes an abusive relationship in which the victim doesn't leave. In the song, the narrator doesn't know if she'll even survive the relationship, but she stays. Some listeners criticized the song, saying it encouraged people to stay in abusive relationships. But "Russian Roulette" is hardly a positive metaphor. If you lose, you die. If you win, you survive, the same reward you get for not playing at all.

"G4L," by James Fauntleroy, explores a revenge fantasy. In the song, somebody crosses the narrator's crew and they go after him. In real life, Rihanna said that she didn't want to bring Brown down. But songs are different than real life. They allow people to ask, "What if?" They allow people to interpret situations in different ways.

Rihanna performs with Ne-Yo at the American Music Awards in Los Angeles on November 18, 2007. He is one of many artists she has collaborated with.

In "Stupid in Love," by Ne-Yo, the narrator turns an accusing finger on herself. She says that she must be an idiot for returning to the wrong guy. She sings that she's doing something stupid even though she's not stupid. In the end, she sings that her dunce cap is off and the guy is the dumb one.

"The Last Song," by Rihanna, is about saying good-bye to a great love. She kept putting off recording this one. Finally, with only twelve hours left to turn in the record, she went to the studio. She faced her own heartbreak. Then she recorded "The Last Song."

Rihanna said her fourth album is named *Rated R* because it explores the different emotions of a situation, just as a movie does. Musically, Rihanna said that *Rated R* has grimier beats than her previous albums.

She described it to *W* magazine in the February 2010 issue as "less synth-y, pop-y, dance-y." She said it also expanded her audience from mainly young people to adults, too.

The change made Evan Rogers nervous. When he heard the album, he said it was like hearing his daughter cuss for the first time. He had concerns about how her audience would react. But he said that when he looked closer, he saw that she was showing a deeper side of herself.

When *Rated R* came out in November 2009, Rihanna could no longer be called a talented but "manufactured" star. She had used what could have been a crushing experience to put out a soul-searching album. *Entertainment Weekly* called it raw and unsettling. The *Chicago Tribune* called "Stupid in Love" devastating. *Rolling Stone* compared her heart-wrenching album to Chris Brown's record, which came out at the same time and which the reviewer criticized for being shallow. Instead of confronting what happened, as Rihanna did, Brown largely ignored it, the reviewer said. The *New York Times* said that through the sadness of Rihanna's album, the craftsmanship still shone through. The *Chicago Sun Times* said the album was a sign of good things to come for Rihanna.

Of course, you can't make all the people happy all the time. The *Washington Post* said Rihanna's earlier upbeat songs were better. (And in fact, one of the biggest hits on the album was "Rude Boy," the kind of lighthearted dance song that originally made her famous.)

Recording music as therapy after the Chris Brown attack, Rihanna released Rated R in 2009. She is pictured here at the album's release party on November 24, 2009, in New York.

RUN THIS TOWN

In Rihanna's interview with Diane Sawyer, she said that Chris Brown had been her first big love.

She added, "We were best friends, so we fell in love with each other. To fall in love with your best friend is really scary. We just fell in love really fast . . . it was a bit of an obsession."

Because of that, she said that leaving Brown was hard. She had to look at her situation as a third person. Would she tell herself to leave? She knew leaving was the right thing to do. She said she was glad that this happened to her because it brought the issue of dating abuse—which is so often a secret—to light.

"This happened to me," she said. "I didn't cause this. I didn't do it. If it can happen to me, it can happen to anyone."

After what she went through, Rihanna got her thirteenth tattoo. It said, "Never a failure; always a lesson." It's written backwards so that she can read it in the mirror. Rihanna had put some things on hold after the attack. Now, with a new album out and with her wounds healing, nothing was stopping her.

In December, she appeared on *Saturday Night Live*. Though she was the musical guest, she offered a hint that she may pursue acting once again. Her performance in the skit "Shy Ronnie" with Andy Samberg became an Internet hit. In it, she becomes frustrated with her duet partner Shy Ronnie, who has a wicked case of stage fright. He miraculously recovers from his stage fright whenever Rihanna leaves the room.

To promote the album, Rihanna also traveled to England, Germany, and France. While in Germany, she heard of a tragedy in her Caribbean homeland. A January 12, 2010, earthquake in Haiti had killed thousands and left many homeless.

Speaking to Oslo TV host Fredrik Skavlan, she said, "In the Caribbean, we think of ourselves as one big family, one country . . . it's like it happened to Barbados." With that in mind, she set to work raising money for her homeland.

On January 20, she went on *Oprah* to perform Bob Marley's "Redemption Song." It was a song she had listened to as a child whenever she suffered hard times, and one she still turns to today. Downloads of the cover raised money for Haiti relief.

Two days later, she performed in London with Jay-Z and U2's Bono and the Edge at Hope for Haiti Now: A Global Benefit for Earthquake Relief. They performed the song "Stranded: Haiti, Mon Amour." The televised event, which featured many musicians and celebrities, raised millions of dollars for Haiti relief.

Rihanna then continued to promote her album and expand her entertainment horizons. She may have missed the 2009 Grammys, but in February of 2010, she returned to accept awards with Jay-Z and Kanye West for best rap song and

RIHANNA'S "BOYS"

Rihanna is known for collaborating with talented musical acts, such as:

Ne-Yo. *Ne-Yo wrote and produced "Russian Roulette," the first single released from* Rated R. *They also collaborated on "Take a Bow," "Unfaithful," and "Hate That I Love You." His own albums include* In My Own Words *and* Year of the Gentleman.

Justin Timberlake. *Timberlake and Rihanna wrote "Cold Case Love" on* Rated R. *He also wrote and appeared in the video "Rehab" with Rihanna. Timberlake, a veteran of* The Mickey Mouse Club *and NSYNC, is now a popular solo artist, known for songs like "Cry Me a River."*

Jay-Z. *Rihanna and Jay-Z earned Grammys for best rap/sung collaborations for "Umbrella" (2008) and "Run This Town," with Kanye West (2010). Jay-Z is a renowned rapper and music mogul.*

best rap/song collaboration for "Run This Town" from Jay-Z's album *Run this Town*. (The song was also used to introduce the Saints and Colts before Super Bowl XLIV.)

That spring, Rihanna performed on *American Idol* and at the Kids' Choice Awards and continued to tour internationally. In July, she was scheduled to begin her U.S. tour, Last Girl on Earth Tour, with Ke$ha and Nicki Minaj in Seattle.

While her professional life sped up, her private life calmed down. The paparazzi had long ago stopped swarming her home, and she was able to live in peace with her best friend, Melissa, and her toy poodle, Oliver. She was able to enjoy friendships—old and new. She

Rihanna and Jay-Z receive awards for best rap song and best rap/sung collaboration for "Run This Town."

liked joking around with her glam team (which does her hair and makeup) and traveling with an entourage that included her managers, beauty professionals, and old friends. Those who had been with her since the beginning of her career, like Jay-Z, continued to be part of her support system.

In the next ten years, Rihanna hopes to find love and have a family. But the past five years of her life have taught her that the future is unpredictable. Instead, she is focused on making beautiful music, innovative fashion statements, and smart business decisions. In that way, she is truly the Good Girl Gone Bad.

TIMELINE

1988 Robyn Rihanna Fenty is born on February 20 in Barbados.

2003 At age fifteen, Rihanna is discovered by music producer Evan Rogers while he and his wife are vacationing in Barbados.

2004 Rihanna tries out for Jay-Z at Def Jam Records and signs to the label.

2005 *Music of the Sun* is released.

2006 *A Girl Like Me* is released.

2007 *Good Girl Gone Bad* is released. Rihanna changes her look.

2008 *Good Girl Gone Bad: Reloaded* is reissued to include "Take a Bow" and "Disturbia"; Rihanna appears in *People*'s Most Beautiful issue.

2009

On February 8, Rihanna is taken to the police station after suffering an attack by her boyfriend at the time, Chris Brown.

November, *Rated R* is released.

November 3, Rihanna is named one of *Glamour*'s women of the year.

November 6, Rihanna appears on *20/20* to talk to Diane Sawyer.

December 5, Rihanna appears on *Saturday Night Live*.

2010

April 8, Rihanna appears on *American Idol*.

2005 *Music of the Sun* (Def Jam Records)
2006 *A Girl Like Me* (Def Jam Records)
2007 *Good Girl Gone Bad* (Def Jam Records)
2008 *Good Girl Gone Bad: Reloaded* (Def Jam Records)
2009 *Rated R* (Def Jam Records)

Rihanna celebrates the success of her album A Girl Like Me, featuring the songs "SOS" and "Unfaithful." Good Girl Gone Bad, her next album, put Rihanna on the map.

ALBUM A musical recording that includes several songs.

BARBADOS The easternmost island in the Caribbean.

CARIBBEAN The sea west of the Atlantic Ocean and south of the Gulf of Mexico. It is bordered by South America, Central America, and the West Indies. The islands of the West Indies are also sometimes referred to as the Caribbean.

COLLABORATION The result of several musical artists working together on a song or album.

DANCEHALL A contemporary style of Caribbean music influenced by reggae.

DATING ABUSE Emotional or physical pain inflicted by a boyfriend, girlfriend, or person on a date.

DEMO A recording that shows the talent and style of a musician.

EDGY Having a sound or look that pushes the envelope.

ENTOURAGE A group of people who work closely with a performance; this can include assistants, management, and hair and makeup people.

GRAMMY An award presented in a variety of music categories by the Recording Academy.

LEUKEMIA Cancer of the blood or bone marrow characterized by an abnormal increase of blood cells.

MOGUL A magnate or powerful business leader.

PLANTATION A large farm or estate where crops are grown for sale in distant markets, rather than local consumption.

POP Having to do with popular culture.

PRODUCER In music, the person who manages the making of an album or demo—from the recording session to the final product. This may include writing or choosing songs, hiring musicians, and finding a record label.

RAP A kind of music that involves chanted words and rock, pop, or R&B beats.

RECORD One or more songs recorded for later listening.

REGGAE A style of music that combines R&B and traditional Jamaican sounds.

SINGLE A song—possibly from an album—released for radio play or Internet downloading.

SOCA A style of Caribbean music that combines soul and calypso.

WEST INDIES The islands that divide the Caribbean Sea and the Atlantic Ocean. They include the Bahamas, Cuba, Haiti and the Dominican Republic, Puerto Rico, and several smaller islands, including Barbados, known as the Lesser Antilles.

Believe Rihanna
c/o Berdon LLP
360 Madison Avenue, 9th Floor
New York, NY 10017
Web site: http://www.believerihanna.com
Believe Rihanna raises money for the medical, educational, social, and financial support of children in need.

Hope for Haiti Now
Web site: http://www.hopeforhaitinow.org
Hope for Haiti Now is an organization that raises money for earth-quake relief in Haiti.

Island Def Jam Recordings
55 Washington Street, Suite 822
Brooklyn, NY 11201
Web site: http://www.islanddefjam.com
Island Def Jam Recordings is a company that makes records.

National Teen Dating Abuse Helpline
(866) 331-9474
Web site: http://www.loveisrespect.org
The National Teen Dating Abuse Helpline is a resource for teens who need help dealing with abuse happening to them or a friend.

Springtide Resources
215 Spadina Avenue, Suite 220
Toronto, ON M5T 2C7
Canada
E-mail: info@womenabuseprevention.com

Web site: http://www.springtideresources.org
Springtide Resources encourages healthy relationships for women
    and teens.

WEB SITES

Due to the changing nature of Internet links, Rosen Publishing has developed an online list of Web sites related to the subject of this book. This site is updated regularly. Please use this link to access the list:

http://www.rosenlinks.com/mega/riha

Bailey, Diane. *Mary J. Blige* (Hip-Hop Biographies). New York, NY: Rosen Publishing Group, 2009.

Frank, Mary Kate. *Rihanna* (Today's Superstars). New York, NY: Gareth Stevens Publishing, 2009.

Heos, Bridget. *Jay-Z* (Hip-Hop Biographies). New York, NY: Rosen Publishing Group, 2009.

Hubbard, Ben. *The History of Pop*. New York, NY: Crabtree Publishing, 2009.

Jones, Jen. *Becoming a Pop Star*. Mankato, MN: Capstone Press, 2008.

Orr, Tamra. *Barbados* (The Caribbean Today). Broomall, PA.: Mason Crest Publishers, 2009.

Petry, Ann. *Tituba of Salem Village*. New York, NY: HarperCollins, 1991.

Silverstein, Herma. *Date Abuse* (Issues in Focus). Berkeley Heights, NJ: Enslow Publishers, 1994.

Solway, Andrew. *Latin America and the Caribbean* (World of Music). Mankato, MN: Heinemann-Raintree, 2008.

ABCNews.com. "Exclusive: Rihanna Speaks Out." *20/20*, November 9, 2009. Retrieved March 29, 2010 (http://abc news.go.com/video/playerIndex?id=9020947).

Choi, Mary H. K. "Cover Girls: Rihanna." Marc Ecko's Complex. Retrieved April 2, 2010 (http://www.complex.com/GIRLS/ Cover-Girls/RIHANNA).

CIA. "Barbados." *The CIA World Factbook*. Retrieved March 30, 2010 (https://www.cia.gov/library/publications/the-world-fact book/geos/bb.html).

Climate Lab. "Barbados." Retrieved March 30, 2010 (http:// climatelab.org/Barbados).

CNN.com. "Photo Appears to Show Bruised Rihanna; Police Probe Leak." February 20, 2009. Retrieved April 12, 2010 (http:// www.cnn.com/2009/SHOWBIZ/Music/02/20/rihanna.photo/ index.html).

Cosmopolitan. "Rihanna Reigns." March 2008. Retrieved April 1, 2010 (http://www.cosmopolitan.com/celebrity/exclusive/ Rihanna-Reigns).

Leonard, Elizabeth. "Rihanna and Chris Brown Are Back Together." *People*, February 27, 2009. Retrieved April 2, 2010 (http:// www.people.com/people/article/0,,20262240,00.html).

Meschino, Patricia. "Montano Aims to Take Soca Music into Mainstream." Reuters, August 24, 2008. Retrieved April 2, 2010 (http://www.reuters.com/article/idUSN2432179620080825).

MTV.com. "Jay-Z." Retrieved April 1, 2010 (http://www.mtv.com/ music/artist/jay_z/artist.jhtml#biographyEnd).

MTV.com. "Rihanna Announces Last Girl on Earth Tour with Ke$ha, Nicki Minaj." April 5, 2010. Retrieved April 2, 2010 (http:// www.mtv.com/news/articles/1635473/20100405/minaj_ nicki.jhtml).

Oprah.com. "Breaking the Dating Violence Cycle." March 12, 2009. Retrieved April 2, 2010 (http://www.oprah.com/relationships/Tyra-Banks-on-Dating-Abuse/11).

People.com. "Rihanna." Retrieved March 28, 2010 (http://www.people.com/people/rihanna/biography).

Rainey, Candice. "Good Girl Gone Great." *Elle*, May 4, 2008. Retrieved April 1, 2010 (http://www.elle.com/Pop-Culture/Cover-Shoots/Good-Girl-Gone-Great/Rihanna-Elle-Magazine-June-20086).

Rao, Anjali. "Rihanna One-on-One." CNN.com, February 24, 2010. Retrieved April 12, 2010 (http://www.cnn.com/2010/SHOWBIZ/Music/02/23/ta.rihanna.blog/index.html).

Rap-Up. "Review Roundup: Rihanna 'Rated R.'" November 23, 2009. Retrieved April 2, 2010 (http://www.rap-up.com/2009/11/23/review-roundup-rihanna-rated-r).

Rolling Stone. "Rihanna: Discography." Retrieved April 1, 2010 (http://www.rollingstone.com/artists/rihanna/discography).

Rosen, Jody. "Rated R." *Rolling Stone*, November 23, 2009. Retrieved April 2, 2010 (http://www.rollingstone.com/reviews/album/30956463/review/31053793/rated_r).

Sandell, Laurie. "Rihanna: Back on Top!" *Glamour*, November 3, 2009. Retrieved April 1, 2010 (http://www.glamour.com/women-of-the-year/2009/rihanna).

Stein, Danielle. "Rihanna." *W*, February 2010. Retrieved March 30, 2010 (http://www.wmagazine.com/celebrities/2010/02/rihanna).

Tangled Roots. "Barbosed." Retrieved April 2, 2010 (http://www.yale.edu/glc/tangledroots/Barbadosed.htm).

INDEX

ABOUT THE AUTHOR

Bridget Heos is the author of twelve young adult nonfiction titles on topics ranging from biographies to science to states. She also writes picture books. Prior to being a children's book author, she was a newspaper reporter and freelance journalist. She lives in Kansas City with her husband and three sons.

PHOTO CREDITS

Cover, pp. 1, 4 Jason Merritt/Getty Images; pp. 3 (top), 18 Valery Hache/AFP/Getty Images; pp. 3 (center), 5 Scott Gries/Getty Images; pp. 3 (bottom), 34 Jeff Kravitz/FilmMagic/Getty Images; pp. 7, 30–31 Johnny Nunez/WireImage/Getty Images; p. 9 Louis Dollagaray/WireImage/Getty Images; p. 12 Gijsbert Hanekroot/Redferns/Getty Images; p. 15 Theo Wargo/WireImage/Getty Images; p. 16 Amanda Edwards/Getty Images; p. 21 John Shearer/WireImage/Getty Images; p. 23 Dimitrios Kambouris/WireImage/Getty Images; p. 25 Lori Shepler/AFP/Getty Images; p. 29 Ethan Miller/Getty Images; p. 38 Eddie Malluk/WireImage/Getty Images.

Designer: Nicole Russo; Editor: Bethany Bryan;
Photo Researcher: Karen Huang